Library of
Davidson College

THE VICTORIAN MUSE

Selected Criticism and Parody of the Period

*A thirty-nine-volume facsimile set
essential to the study of one of the most
prolific periods in English literature*

*Edited by
William E. Fredeman, Ira Bruce Nadel, John F. Stasny*

A Garland Series

Poems Inspired by Certain Pictures at the Art Treasures Exhibition, Manchester

The Laughter of the Muses

Garland Publishing, Inc.
New York & London
1986

821.08
P7441

For a complete list of the titles in this series
see the final pages of this volume.

The facsimile of *Poems Inspired by Certain Pictures* has been made from a copy in the British Library; that of *Laughter of the Muses* is from a copy in the Yale University Library.

Library of Congress Cataloging-in-Publication Data

Main entry under title:

Poems inspired by certain pictures at the Art Treasures Exhibition, Manchester.

(The Victorian muse)
Reprint (1st work). Originally published: Manchester, 1857.
Reprint (2nd work). Originally published: Glasgow : T. Murray, 1869.
1. English poetry—19th century. 2. Satire, English.
3. Painting, English—Poetry. 4. Preraphelitism—Poetry.
I. Waring, J. B. (John Burley), 1823–1875. Poems inspired by certain pictures at the Art Treasures Exhibition, Manchester. 1986. II. Laughter of the muses. 1986. III. Series.
PR1195.S3P6 1986   821'.8'08   85-25356
ISBN 0-8240-8624-4 (alk. paper)

Design by Bonnie Goldsmith

The volumes in this series are printed on acid-free, 250-year-life paper.

Printed in the United States of America

POEMS

INSPIRED BY CERTAIN PICTURES

AT THE

ART TREASURES EXHIBITION,

MANCHESTER,

BY

TENNYSON LONGFELLOW SMITH,

OF

CRIPPLEGATE WITHIN,

EDITED BY HIS FRIEND, THE AUTHOR OF "THORNS & THISTLES."

ILLUSTRATED BY THE HON. BOTIBOL BAREACRES;

AND

𝔇𝔢𝔡𝔦𝔠𝔞𝔱𝔢𝔡,

WITH PROFOUND ADMIRATION AND AWE,

TO

THAT GREATEST OF MODERN POETS, PHILOSOPHERS,
ARTISTS, ART-CRITICS, AND AUTHORS,

THE IMMORTAL BUSKIN.

MANCHESTER:
SOLD AT THE BOOK-STALL OF THE EXHIBITION,
AND BY ALL RESPECTABLE BOOKSELLERS.

The Awakened Conscience

POEMS.

The Awakened Conscience.

BY HOLMAN HUNT.

Now, really, Mr. Holman Hunt, this can't be called correct,
And in your more developed stage what *are* we to expect?
Some things, there are, you know, *bon ton* don't recognise at all,
I'm really quite surprised that you should paint a what-d'ye-call!

"Madam; the painter do not blame with too severe a tongue,
(The creature from the canvas speaks) I'm neither fair nor young.
And Mr. Hunt, with moral aim, would frighten every gent
From taking up with such as me, on wickedness when bent.

"My hollow cheeks, my starting eyes, my red dishevelled hair,
Should horror strike in those bad men who've known what once
    they were;
Whilst Frederic, grinning by my side, a swell, a fool, a muff,
To sicken all right-minded girls is surely quite enough.

"I own my windows don't, in fact, look on the church-yard sod,
But Mr. H. would have it so, being obstinate and odd.
'Twould give such force, he said — was full of meaning, dark
    and sad;
And really, as he's managed it, it doesn't look so bad!

" As for the cat, I must observe, my Lulu, pretty pet,
Though often eyeing Dickey's cage, has never harmed it yet;
Still, it's a good idea; and so's the scarf around me thrown;
Its colours bright serve well to show how pallid I am grown.

" I've lived and loved (some years ago) in halls of dazzling light,
And heard my lovers serenade oft in the stilly night;
But, love not, for the thing you love may die, or will not last;
And if there is one flower that fades, 'tis the memory of the past!*

" So, Madam, please to moderate the rancour of your tongue;
For, as I have observed before, I'm neither fair nor young.
Yet let me hope the whole effect,—my features wan and pale,
At least may point a moral, if they can't adorn a tale."

---

* The beautiful and ingenious manner in which the burdens of these popular and truly soul-inspired poems are introduced by Mr. T. L. S. deserves especial notice. Observe, also, the wide extent of his reading in our poetic literature, evidenced in the sudden reference to an old and simple melo-drama at the opening of the succeeding verse, and to reading of a still more serious and recondite nature in the last line of the same stanza.—*Ed.*

The Hireling Shepherd.

BY H. HOLMAN HUNT.

Oh! jolly young countryvolk be we,
Full o' life, an blood, an jollity;
If I do whack Poll, why Poll do whack me,
      Darn humbug, zez I.

I do zgorn your lord and your parsing too,
With their pasty chops and their hullabaloo,
For I lies on the grass, and ha'n't nuthun to do,—
      Poll minds the zheep.

Whilst Mr. Hunt my fiziog draws,
An told m as how h' wuz quite surpraws
T' zee zo much blood in any chap's jaws,
      And guv me a guinea.

Not as I'm gwoing to tell to yew
Whot with that guinea I means for to dew;
But darn'd if I don't have a spree or tew
      At the Pig and Whistle.

And Poll, thof her have that fancy lamb
As I can't abide, shall have a cram,
And zo, zur, its much obleeged I am.
      (Sotto voce.)   Bain't her a zoft, Poll? *

---

* My friend, T. L. S., gives proof, in this little poem, of that judgment, refinement, and exquisite taste which can touch on the coarsest subject and yet escape the acousation of grossness. A sweet sound is drawn from a rude rural reed; and his originality—his sense of the appropriate—is evinced in the peculiar and difficult idiom he has chosen for this effort of his genius, viz., that of Somersetshire, noted for its red-cheeked clowns and green apples. N.B.—In the racy dialect of the county it is pronounced Zoommurzshutzhyer. We remark, also, the last lingering glimmer of a long lost and deeply regretted age of chivalry and romance, in the fact that all things are indiscriminately known as "*her*" in this county.

The Two Gentlemen of Verona.

BY HOLMAN HUNT.

SANG in times which now are olden,*
   Fast by Avon's flowing stream,
Many a legend, weird and golden—
   Things which are not what they seem.†

Shakspere of the wide evangel,
   Him of Godlike soul profound;
Of all poets chief archangel;
   And amongst them this is found :—‡

Sir Proteus and Sir Valentine
   Loved two ladies passing well;
One, of Milan's princely line;
   The other, a Verona belle.

'T would take a long time to explain
   All the windings of the plot;
How well our Shakspeare lays the train,—
   Who did wrong and who did not.

Till within a bosky § wood,
   All the four are met at last;

---

* † The affectionate reverence displayed by T. L. S. in these touching and gentle references to the most beautiful leaves in the laurel crown of his Transatlantic godfather, must affect every feeling heart with pleasure.

‡ The bold transition from the vivid description of Shakspere to the subject in hand, forms, perhaps, one of the most striking instances on record of how genius can deal with the figure, "Aposiopesis."

§ That the study of T. L. S. has not been confined to our modern warblers is proved by this Miltonian phrase. We may add that Milton no doubt introduced the sweet expression from Italy, in which language it is an interesting fact that "bosco" means a wood or forest The charge of vulgarism has been brought against our author for using this word, but is it not evident that this particular "bosky" does not apply to a gross excess in strong drinks; for, although many a stick may get tipsy, who ever heard of a wood being drunk? The charge is preposterous.

The two Gentlemen of Verona

Each one in a different mood,
  Sir Proteus on his knee, aghast!

Above him, brave Sir Valentine,
  Armour-clad, and knock'd of knee,
Looking mighty proud and fine,
  Has stept out from behind a tree.

Lady Sylvia kneels beside him—
  Daughter of proud Milan's line;
For Proteus, she cannot abide him,
  But loves her own dear Valentine.*

As for Proteus, recreant knight,
  Well may he hang down his head,
And hold his neck with grip so tight,
  A crick in which near strikes him dead.

Behaving thus so very sadly
  Unto Sylvia and his friend,
And to Julia just as badly—
  She who loves him to the end!

Julia rests against a tree,
  Disguised like a youthful page;
And is not sorry thus to see
  Things arrive at such a stage.

So she proves that she is Julia,
  And, indeed, no page at all;
Proteus, this was done to fool ye;
  You must feel uncommon small!

Uncommon small! of course he does;
  So, after being duly harried,

---

* With the conscious sense of truly powerful genius, my friend does not shrink from impressing into the service of his Muse the most popular expressions of our national poetry; and this easy simplicity brings to our remembrance, in this particular instance, one of the most charming and palpitating days of the year, and an old, old custom, happily not yet trodden out of England by the iron hoof of steam.

Each gives each a loving kiss,
    And all four are shortly married.

Hunt, with great power of imitation,
    Hath limned the poet's pleasant story;
Still, if we ask some explanation,
    Be not offended, we implore ye.

Why, then, is Sylvia on her knees?
    And Proteus, too, on one knee slid? *
And why such *very* little trees
    Behind which Valentine was hid?

And why are both the ladies fair?
    Why's Proteus like a Sussex clod?
Why have they all such curious hair?
    Why's Julia's figure made so odd?

But, ask no more what may be meant;
    Remember, life is but a dream;
He doubtless wish'd to represent
    Things which are not what they seem.

---

* For the justice of this pungent criticism the intelligent reader is referred to any edition of that great dramatist known by our brethren across the Channel as the "Divine Williams."

Claudio & Isabella

Claudio and Isabella.

BY HOLMAN HUNT.

" What's the matter, what's the matter?*
    Have you pains in your inside?
Why do your teeth thus loudly clatter?
    Tell the worst that may betide.

" Why's your body thus distorted?
    What's the matter with your heel?
Pray, by me, now, be exhorted—
    Tell me what it is you feel.

" Is it what I just have told you?
    Claudio, do not fear to fall,
" For with both hands thus I hold you
    Fast and tight against the wall.

" Life, I know, is very pleasant;
    Death a very dubious riddle;
Yet, remember, you're no peasant,
    But part your hair straight down the middle.

" Yes, your hair is nobly parted,
    And you wear a noble's dress;
So, prithee, don't be chicken-hearted—
    To such weakness don't confess.

---

* We believe that a poem by the late amiable but deluded Wordsworth commences somewhat in this style; but no charge of plagiarism should or could be justly brought against my dear friend on this account, since the opening expression is one of that class which may naturally occur to all poets of genius anyway "hors de ligne."

"Think what life is without honor;
  Don't be looking at your feet;
Boldly, bravely, look upon her—
  Death I mean—and think it sweet."

Thus spake fair, young Isabella
  To her brother—soon to die,
Because he's been a gay young fellah,*
  And broke the laws most flagrantly.

Measure for Measure is the play;
  The which, if you have never read,
Its perusal, any day,
  Will prove how vice is punished.

But pray don't think there's any reason
  Why thus the picture we explain;
The subject you at once would seize on,
  And own 'tis Shakspeare o'er again.

For is not Claudio inly writhing,
  Distraught with shame and puling fear,
With basest thoughts still vainly striving,
  And trying to squeeze out a tear?

Whilst she, the maiden, chaste and proud,
  Regards him with superb disdain,
As, with indignant words and loud,
  She bids him be a man again.

And Hunt, of genius most Titanic,
  A very Shakspeare of the brush,
In each spectator's soul strikes panic,
  And makes all coward spirits blush.

---

* We own we are doubtful how far a poet—even such a poet as T. L. S.—is justified in altering the proper spelling of the most trivial word in our beloved and nervous language. We would only remark that in the best society "fellow" is *always* pronounced *fellah*. In that society T. L. S. was born, was nurtured, and has always moved as one of its most distinguished ornaments. Need we say more?

Thank heaven! we live in glorious days;
   Poor Raffaelle seems a blundering child
Beside our Hunts and our Millais,
   Whilst Rembrandt's meaningless and wild.

These soul-less infants of the past,
   With all their sensual, pagan crew,
Could they re-live, would stand aghast
   At sight of what *our* youths can do.

Convent Thoughts.

BY C. A. COLLINS.

GREAT is the power of the painter, wonderful garden of greenness,
And sweet is the sense of seclusion, though millions of lilies and roses
Here twine and spring up and are tangled—at least, if not tangled, they might be,
Were it not that the hand of the gardener hath carefully grouped all their beauties.
Verdant the grass which, beneath thee, looks like a carpet of green baize;
Verdant the bushes and berries, springing up in most excellent order;
Verdant the wall at the back, too, with many a year's growth of something;*
And verdant thy thoughts, oh, young spirit, which, shrouded beneath that grey habit,
(Straight in a line doth it fall each side of thy delicate figure),
Holdest in one of thy hands, so tiny and fragile and bony,
Passion's bright flower of the south, mystical, bursting with meaning.
And if you look up to the sky, or the top of the brick wall beneath it;

---

* My friend, with that honesty of soul which characterises him, disdains to particularise where he is uncertain,—to bounce, as it is vulgarly termed, when he is ignorant. No, he owns his ignorance with a noble candour. We cannot assist the reader ourselves as to the name of the plant, but it is *not* ivy, as we have heard stated.

Or if you should pitch on the "something," or fall on the leaves and the flowers,
Or let your thoughts lie on the grass, or tumble down into the water,
Or fasten upon the poor nun, who looks so unusually meagre,
You feel all the power of the artist—wonderful power of the artist—
Who, with nothing but colour and brushes, can fill all your being with sadness,
Such as the pretty plants feel when they shiver and sigh at the twilight.
So we stagger awe-stricken away, with a heavy, a tear-burdened bosom,
For we see that a something too holy, too lovely for mere human beings,
Is hidden beneath that grey robe, and we totter on tremblingly forward.

Autumn Leaves.

BY MILLAIS.

GRANDLY great, oh painter of the bright hues dying,
Art thou; and very full of meaning is the sighing
Beauty of thy "autumn leaves," which now, not dancing
On dull Novembrial boughs, through hoar frost glancing,
But here, all speckled, dank, plague-spotted, rotten,
Into a festering mass of loathsome filth are gotten,
Liker damp sculls within a sepulchre; the whilst, around,
Four human spirits stand upon the ground.
Fair children they, well versed in life's sad mystery,
With eight great eyes explain the history,*
Whilst redolent of thought, unto the thinking mind,
The last faint glow of sunset sweeps across behind.

---

* It is true that the eight eyes are not *all* fixed on the spectator, and, as it were, speaking words of deep and melancholy import to him. The explanation of the sad tale symbolised in this painting is, however, no less made clear to us by the eyes of the industrious domestic and of the sweet and innocent little prattler to the right, who sees nothing more before her—like many an uneducated child of longer growth—than a heap of dirty damp leaves.

Autumn Leaves

Burd Helen

Burd Helen.

BY WYNDAS.

Burd Helen had a radiant face
    When dancing on the green;
A prettier girl at ball or race,
Regatta, fair, or steeple-chase,
    Was surely never seen.

But ah! no sun but has its speck,
    No sky but has its cloud;
My milk-white horse has got a fleck,*
And accidents we little reck
    May happen in a crowd.

Sure never was a bird so gay—
    So strong upon the wing;
Yet rainy proved her summer day,
And she would neither sport nor play,
    Nor pretty ditties sing.

The reason why, was (so I'm told),
    A little heart affair;—
She met a Templar brave and bold,
Who turned out cruel, false, and cold,
    And for her did not care.

So, reckless of his good renown,
    He mounted on his horse,
And said he should go back to town;
On which, she went and changed her gown,
    And followed him, of course.

---

* It is useless seeking to conceal what will be clear to every observant reader—that my friend was of a sporting turn; and, indeed, a thorough man of the world, alas!

He rode, and he rode, and he rode, and he rode,*
  As swift as any stag;
But she ran after, nimble-toed,
Through hedge and ditch, through slush and slode, †
  As fast as legs could wag.

So on they coursed, till close of day,
  When they came to a common drear,
All jagged with flints—white, blue, and grey,—
And furze and brambles, which hurt, they say,
  When your feet are almost bare.

And after that was a river deep—
  Might frighten e'en Leander; ‡
Still to his side the Burd did keep,
Swearing that in the stream she'd leap,
  Like Cæsar or Alexander. §

But, ah! this false, this cruel knight
  Was not a whit dismayed;
He grinn'd, and said, this will stop your flight,
So, Madam, I wish you a very good night.
  I wish I had him flay'd!

If I could gain so true a love,
  How happy should I be!
Alas, no star that shines above,
And twinkles bright in heaven's alcove,
  Can farther be from me.

---

* It may occur to some that there is a certain similarity between this truly graphic line and one in the celebrated and popular poem of "Lord Bateman," but I have the best authority for stating that my beloved friend never read that somewhat coarse effusion.

† In vain will the philologistic reader turn to Johnson and others for this word. It is a purely old Anglo-Saxon expression, with which T. L. S. has been recently favoured through the medium of the departed and lamented spirit of Alfred the Great.

‡ And, let me add, even impulsive, unhappy Byron.

§ This allusion serves to prove that my honoured friend was as familiar with the history of a long-past age as with the more pleasing writers of our own times.

And now, to tell you all the rest,—
  How poor Burd Helen fared,
Or what befel that knight so bad,
Or how they both went raving mad,—
  I'm really not prepared.

But in a ballad, quaint and old,
  You'll find it sweetly written,
And if you are, what I make bold
To think you are, you'll spend your gold
  And buy it, like a Briton.*

Thine, Wyndas, is a glorious name,
  New added to the list
Of England's chosen imps of fame,
Who put all painters else to shame,
  Wherever they exist.

So wonderfully do you know
  How metal's laid in loads,
The nation (gratitude to show),
Should constitute you, here below,
  Surveyor of our roads! †

---

* This smacks, indeed, of the true old English spirit; does it not?
† Palmam qui meruit ferat!

B

Pre-Raffaelleite Chorus.

Air:—"The One-Horse Chaise."

Oh, we live in wretched days, there are few whom we can praise,
Save the happy band of brothers who "Pre-Raffaelleite" are called;
All the rest will come to grief, with no hope of relief,
And by our prophet, Buskin, will be regularly mauled.

Still no more will we say, of the painters of to-day,
Who, if they only join our ranks, may yet perhaps be saved;
But for Raffaelle and his crew, we will pink them through and through,
And Buskin's name in blood upon their souls shall be engraved.

That Raffaelle was a fool, like all others of his school,
Without sentiment or soul,—a sensual heathen brute;
But although he has a name, yet Buskin soon his fame
Shall scratch and tear to tatters, and trample under foot.

As for wretched Buonarotti, so contorted, coarse, and dotty,
Such a humbug diabolical has never yet been known;
An emissary from Hades, from whom gentlemen and ladies
Should turn in proper horror, and entirely disown!

There's that satyr, J. Romano; that immoral Tiziano;
Giorgione, Tintoretto, Guido,—demons, one and all,
Whom we loathe, abhor, detest; and we swear to take no rest
Till we dance upon their monuments, both great and small.

Oh, Rembrandt's simply bosh; and Ruben's actual slosh;
And those who dare say otherwise are fools, and dogs, and slaves.
Vandyke, Ostade, and Snyders, with the squad of Dutch outsiders,
Were a set of heartless, pagan, drunken, muddle-headed knaves.

As for poor old Claude Lorraine, Buskin makes it very plain
That a muff more unartistic we couldn't well conceive;
Whilst dull Salvator Rosa is a "maladetta cosa,"
And they and all who follow them are doomed without reprieve.

The Poussins and Le Brun, we will show you very soon,
Were nothing more than pagans of the deepest, blackest dye,
In fact, throughout the century, to take an oath we venture, ye
Will find no Christian sentiment, or anything that's high.

And every single Spaniard is ridiculously mannered;
Velasques and Murillio, with Zurbaran as well;
Old Cano and El Greco, would a pretty party make, oh!
In a place that mayn't be mentioned, as I need not tell.

In that *place* they all have got, let us hope, a fiery lot,
For the dark artistic crimes which they committed here on earth,
Whilst we shout with might and main, till the heavens vibrate again,
That High Art in Great Britain has at last been brought to birth.

And Buskin swears that now, if your knee you do not bow,
And humbly, to the Genius of this Infant so divine,
He will give you such a slashing,—such a mashing, crashing, thrashing,
As befits a set of donkeys, or a herd of filthy swine.

So, you see, we must be right; and, having put you in a fright,
Go, burn your stupid ancient daubs, and come to us to school;
Then perhaps you may, some day, find out the proper way
To look on Art and Nature, and cease to be a fool.

THE
LAUGHTER OF THE MUSES:

A Satire

ON

THE REIGNING POETRY OF 1869.

GLASGOW:
THOMAS MURRAY & SON, 31, BUCHANAN STREET
1869.

PREFACE.

THE reader of the following verses is desired to consider them not so much an attack as a defence. Books may be viewed as armies of words, marshalled in orderly or confused array by chapters, their generals. They are sent forth to do battle with the words already entrenched in the memories of men. It is surely a legitimate warfare when these rise up in self-defence. The impartial public looking on is the judge of their success or failure.

The ideas of general and particular are sometimes better understood by such a mode of conducting literary operations. Those who already understand these ideas will understand the design of this treatise, and those who do not may learn if they will. The author would simply say here, that there is a general ALFRED TENNYSON and a not quite so general ROBERT BROWNING; and that there is a particular Mr. TENNYSON and a particular Mr. BROWNING. He endeavours in these pages to give reasons for taking exception with the two former alone.

Such trifling matters as the alteration of a word here and there in different editions by the writers animadverted on, are perhaps now and then overlooked; but this is no great hardship, as their productions are here looked upon as a whole, and the author hopes he has been able to show that they are destitute of those redeeming qualities which lead all liberal-minded men to pass over little defects, such as involuntary repetitions of the same thoughts and unavoidable adoptions of the same words. But when these little defects constitute in fact the bulk of their merit; when these repetitions and adoptions are unmistakeable evidences of scanty resources, they are treated without mercy; they deserve to be exposed, because it makes simple, unpretending people imagine that no more can be said, that all the fields of thought have been cut and gleaned, and that all the worlds of light have yielded up their secrets to astronomical poets, when it may turn out that their eyes have never seen them at all.

THE LAUGHTER OF THE MUSES.

PART I.

THE
LAUGHTER OF THE MUSES.

PART I.—ROBERT BROWNING.

Long had the Sisters Nine their blest employ
In groves remote pursued without annoy,
Till on a day young Cupid thither strayed
To rest himself within their pleasant glade.
His merry presence made them gay and brisk,
And waked in each great longing for a frisk.
With their young guide they wandered thro' the land,
All bent on pleasure, aye at Love's command.
Swiftly they moved along, to greet the Spring's
Approach in youth's attire, who with her brings
The minstrels, flowers, and blossoms for the earth,
That make it seem the chosen home of mirth.

They saw and listened with delight together;
Love filled their souls, as in the pleasant weather
They freely lived, and wandered where they would;
Their freedom was of peace and love the food.
They touched at London on their southward way,
And on the brow of "Cornhill" for a day
Remained, for CUPID'S eyes, heavy with sleep
And weariness, could scarcely open keep.
One took him to her bosom, where the pug
Lay with a willing mind, in comfort snug.
They hearkened to the roar of Babylon,
That rose up all around, and fell upon
Their gentle sense with little harm at all,
For there is nothing can their ears appal.

While thus the Muses rested on the sward,
At the hillfoot below they clearly heard
A middle-aged scribbler, whose delight
In song resembles "pudding,"* use his might,

---

* *Vide* the "Cornhill Magazine" of February, 1869.

As after dinner he would write a line,
To cry, "BROWNING in Eighteen sixty-nine."
The listening virgins to each other smiled,
Then burst into loud laughter; Love's gay child,
In his delicious couch from sleep awoke,
His quick ear startled by the sudden shock
Of merriment, and asked his lovely nurse—
"What's this?"   "We laugh, sweet child, at
   BROWNING'S verse."
"Who's BROWNING?" he replied; "I have not heard
'Mongst all my English loves of such a bard."
"Therefore we laugh," ERATO made reply:
"How mad is he, who thought to pass thee by,
And yet expect to have a poet's voice,
To tell the world what made his life rejoice!
Oft hath he sought our countenance to seek,
Returning to the charge from week to week,
But aye we gave him a refusal grim;
With one accord we said we'd none of him.
MELPOMENE for him would never wake;
His sprawling rhymes made us in haste forsake

The windows, and behind the arras hide,
Till with his hopeless songs, which sense defied,
He'd go away, and leave us for a while."
"'Twas fitting," CUPID answered with a smile,
" To turn him off, who, asking not my aid,
Dared to approach a Heaven-inspired maid:"
" There," cried the Muse, " he comes this way again,
To give us all the strains his weary pen
Hath made him; see, he smiles and reads,
And reads and smiles: his must be happy deeds
Of thought that to his face bring such delight.
How sad we cannot join with him, poor wight!
But not one note of harmony has he
In all his columns long, that we can see."
" Let's hear," said CUPID, laughing, " this new air,"
Stroking with his fat hand her yellow hair:
" *The Ring and the Book;* how," cried the Boy, " what's
  this?"
And rising up, snatched from the Muse a kiss;
" He brings the *Ring* to take you for his bride,
Storming your heart with his loud-shouting pride;

The *Book* contains the service to be read,
When you to this dull ancient shall be wed."
"Never," the Muse replied, "shall I my favours
Bestow on him; my purpose never wavers
Of bidding him begone once and for all;
Tell him to 'turn his face round to the wall,
And bid the world good-night; in a sound sleep
Lie till the trumpet's blowing;' let him keep
His dull pearls in his casket, there's not one
That I shall ever care to look upon.
He calls them pearls, I know not what they are,
But this I know, all proper taste they mar.
We have a page at home, 'a harmless drudge,'
Who toils through all his books without a grudge,
And we have promised soon to hear the sense
He makes of them; come, sisters, let us hence.
Thou, too, Love's child, return with us to-day,
And give thine audience to this little play."
Up rose the maidens, CUPID running on
Before, and turning ever and anon

His smiling face round on the graceful band,
Who leisurely him followed, hand in hand.
Their motions were delight, their glances joy,
That answered well the gladness of the boy.
At sunset coming to the wicket gate,
Where in rich garments nine young pages wait,
They passed into the grove; on to her bower
ERATO led them, saying, "Here for an hour,
In the soft twilight, sisters, let us linger."
She beckoned on her page with lifted finger,
Who with a measured step came forward then,
Leaving the eight behind; they, happy men,
Their service ended for that day, the green
Now sought to sport and frolic, for each queen
Makes all obedience pleasant in their eyes;
It is to them but freedom in disguise,
A masquerade where they meet ladies fair,
For whom they would hardships and dangers bear.
Meanwhile the favoured page before the choir
Stood up and sang, with laughter for his lyre:

THE LAUGHTER OF THE MUSES.

"O royal ladies, now I may not seek
Thanks for this favour in fit words to speak,
In place whereof I would at once begin
The pleasant task for which ye've called me in.
Innumerable rhymes from one man's tongue
Should yield some joy; alas! not for a bung
To shut up BACCHUS' mirth will they suffice;
All Comedy on such a diet dies,
Much less can they unto your virgin ears
Give ravishment; no bliss of youthful years
Perfumes his fancies, they are dull with age,
And cold enough Love's ardour to assuage.
Love falls asleep when he begins to read,
For there is nothing at his board can feed,
And Love must eat or sleep; the table's bare,
Most comfortless; of hunger, man, beware;
All you possess just now is old and sour,
And soon perhaps you may not have the power
To buy the bread that's ever fresh and sweet,
Which pampered taste makes you so loath to eat.

He did not write for ROBERT BROWNING's sake,
But that he might a 'British public' shake
Who 'like' him not.   Pshaw! 'liking's' not the thing
To make a poet over others king.

"This man's presumption has but small excuse,
For he has found that very few will choose
To read his volumes, yet he perseveres
In thinking he the poet's impress bears.
Now through each weary page you'll search in vain
For any rhyme sung by his busy brain
That you would care to think upon and cherish;
Strong is the wish to let it quickly perish
From the remembrance, it doth so offend
The guests already there; they quickly send
To limbo this intruding bore, who speaks
For the same reason that a vessel leaks.
A nature loosely constituted soon
Makes itself known; he sees the sun and moon,
And straight concludes they ask from him a song;
He goes to perpetrate the greatest wrong

They ever yet received—speaks painfully,
And leaves them wondering at his vanity,
His emptiness of clear and full delight,
That most resembles dreams absurd by night;
And so 'tis fit we laugh them out of mind,
That we may not day's common-sense make blind.
We want him not, for all the past remains,
And BROWNING is a blockhead for his pains,
Who tries to stuff his crudities in front,
When all the world shouts loudly to him, 'Dont!'
His verses on each page hang like to crabs
Upon a string, collected by old drabs,
Who at this age's low poetic tide
Wade out in petticoats of learned pride,
And, stooping, gather up all refuse cast
By its full flow in generations past.
He cannot write; then wherefore should he try?
Let him find pleasure with his silent eye,
Put hands into his pockets, let no more
His fingers itch to open the barred door

Of language, he hath failed so long,
Let him retire and listen to the song
Of those who had free access to the seats
Where Thought with Melody right gladly meets.
As unto them he hearkens he will learn
True sense from trite sensation to discern;
When once he learns he'll sink into the dust,
And ever after leave his pen to rust.

In *Give a Rouse*, we clearly see good sack spilt,
For there he spoils the rhyme, 'This is the house that
 Jack built.'
I'd rather spend my shillings on stewed prunes
Than on what he calls cavalierly *Cavalier Tunes*.

The Spanish Cloister he would famous make
By a soliloquy that no one spake,
And never would, until it fell from him;
Still it may help to line a beaver's rim,
Which he himself may wear for aught he knows,
For who can tell where useless writing goes?

His rhyming he hath learned from HUDIBRAS,
Where such rhymes answer well; but what we pass
In BUTLER, has in BROWNING not a grace,
For when he jokes, he turns awry his face.
We laugh at him as at a juggler's tricks;
Nothing has he admiring love to fix.
He writes for Rhyme's poor sake, that feels ashamed
At being placed so high, and deep thought named;
Good as a slave, 'tis hateful as a master;
And BROWNING'S nothing but a poetaster.

"What he has thoughtless called *Dramatic Lyrics*
Are prudish Poetry's chronic hysterics.
In the *Flight of the Duchess* the lady still flies,
And no one can catch her, however he tries.
Dear sir, as a man, I shall 'love you for ever,'
But to love you as poet quite vain's my endeavour.
In *The Glove* he must spoil THOMAS CAMPBELL'S good line,
And says 'Distance all value enhances' is mine.
For him this wise reflection was not meant,
Or to a distance he his songs had sent!

Would he had long ere this his *Garden Fancies* turned
To better use, and, like the parchment book he spurned
And buried in a plum-tree, had consigned
The plaguy pedantry of his weak mind
To some such hiding-place, for 'tis unfit
Beside legitimate and pleasant thought to sit,
And we impatiently cry to him, 'Zooks!
The land is too much cumbered with your books!'
Words are his stock-in-trade, which are a drug
In every market; men their shoulders shrug
At the raw country bard, with such a load,
Calling for customers, in accents broad.

" Boldness and Ignorance know no alarms,
And for the thoughtless both alike have charms;
But chiefly Ignorance, which saves them wholly
From patient work's distressful melancholy;
Fearless they plunge into the deepest seas,
Where they have room to flounder at their ease;
Conceptions huge, like whales, are ever theirs,
At which the universal ocean stares;

Not small fry they, to be content with hearing
In depths unknown, they must be ever rearing
Their heads on high, and blowing water-spouts,
To call forth from the rest admiring shouts,
Till a swift harpoon pierces blubber through,
And turneth up their helplessness to view;
Then high and dry they're stretched upon the sands,
To be dissected by a hundred hands.
Self-constituted arbiters of taste,
Their words are scattered o'er Pride's burning waste,
Where no streams flow to overcome the drought
With which their meanings gasp, a hopeless rout.

"Somewhere he says, ' My SHELLEY,' though of all
Live writers, such a name again to call
Back to the light from the melodious past,
'Tis certain BROWNING should have been the last;
For music is as distant from his ears
As SHELLEY was from calm and happy years.
But TENNYSON of SHAKSPERE says the same
In a strange song 'tis better not to name

Just now, as we are thinking by-and-by
With him on his clipped wings to seek to fly.

" From his *Dramatic Lyrics* turn we now
To what he *Dramas* with undaunted brow
Shrinks not from designating; where we've proof
How he will never keep his hands aloof
From anything, but boldly rushes in
To drown all happy utterance with his din.
He prays before the shrine of an old name,
Convinced that there he finds successful fame.
Of 'Dramas' he now drinketh many a dram,
Led to his ruin like an unthinking lamb.

" This platitude you in *Sordello* buy:
' Plucker of amaranths grown beneath God's eye.'
Where else, I wonder, would he find his flowers?
We are not slow t' admit his prosy powers
' With individuality are stamped,'
But, O! how shall we say, how stiff and cramped!

He tries to make his foot find room enough
In Cinderella's slipper; voice so gruff
Seems a hoarse whisper when it sinks to song,
And CUPID makes have bad dreams all night long.
The hideous 'Fee, faw, fum, bubble and squeak,'
Makes him resolve a vengeance dire to wreak
On BROWNING, who thus dares disturb his peace,
Nor at his nightmare groans the clamour cease;
Still 'Bang, whang, whang,' resounds the poet's drum,
And 'Tootle-te-tootle' his fife; O! when shall come
The end of his mind's pain, that on him falls
At no 'uncertain fits;' he daily bawls
A steady inspiration, till the 'wedding guest'
His eye attempts to hold, sternly demands a rest.
For who can bear to listen to this trash,
This toppling thought, 'Behold, from out their crash'?
Doth not this sentence to the heavens soar:
'God's justice, and no less—that, and no more'?
A universal motto for mankind,
That with its vast conception fills the mind,

And we in its refreshment sharing justly,
' Go boldly, go serenely, go augustly.'

" In *Paracelsus* this before me hove,
' Power, ānd with mūch power, ālways mūch more lōve;'
Just like the youth who would to JOHNSON come
And utter forth of all his thoughts the sum,
Till JOHNSON taught him thus his awkward gait:
' Put yōur knife ānd your fōrk acrōss your plāte.'

" In *Strafford* who will say a poet sings?
Only the names, you'll find, are pleasant things,
As HAMPDEN, HOLLIS, PYM, WENTWORTH, and VANE;
All else is like to thrashing with a cane
Roundhead, to make Sir Cavalier speak out,
But dumb he still continues, never doubt,
For as he tells us, just as ' life is hard
To take from England,' so out of this bard.

" Still persecutes he peace with *Pippa Passes*,
And tries to petrify all daring lasses;

Of one he speaks what none that ever trod
This earth before had thought of saying, 'My God!
Those morbid, olive, faultless shoulder-blades'—
(Students of medicine, speak ye thus of maids?)
'I should have known there was no blood beneath.'
Of many cutting words men God their sheath
Have made, but this requires a BROWNING'S nerve!
There's not enough in the whole book to serve
For a green-grocer's garden-plot of wit,
When of an evening in the sun he'ld sit.
Take one more look before we turn away:
Surely when 'Ottima' is made to say
Unto her guilty paramour, when she
Dies with him, 'There, there, both deaths presently,'
Reality is dead and in its grave,
And BROWNING, like the Witch of Endor, comes to wave
His harmless wand above it, but in vain,
For out of sight it wishes to remain;
We rather think that if it once should rise
'Twould frighten him, and make his quill more wise.

The pages following make us farther see
' His typified invincibility '
To the attacks unconscious ignorance
With ceaseless fury makes on him; its glance
Can no more terrify his vaulting mind,
Whose clattering Pegasus hears nought behind.

" He speaks with silly, superficial twang,
And he alone, for character doth hang
Upon the gallows, where no understanding
Is given it, all the crowd around demanding
Its dying speech, when words, like ropes, have choked
All utterance. A hangman's always mocked
For choosing such a trade. A vacant mind
Is but a turnkey to the ill-inclined;
Sometimes he bursts his fetters with a jerk,
And rushing on him, strikes his hidden dirk
Deep in the gaoler's thigh! he hastens to the door,
And makes for once a real and life-like roar;
But none will take compassion on his pain,
So there he stands exposed to laughter's rain,

That falls upon his bald pate all day long;
Where now is all the bravery of his song?

"*Blot in the Scutcheon* is past remedy;
Its thoughts, its words, its verse most inky be;
'Twas ink made this from left to right hand post:
'Or bringing Austin to pluck up that most;'
'Twas guilty ink made the white pages kiss
'Ill-timed, misplaced, attempted smartnesses.'
His 'gush in golden-tinted plenty down
Her neck's rose-misted marble,' is the crown
Of taste preposterous, which he may wear
Who makes a cascade of a woman's hair.

"Of *Luria* but little needs be said,
For there is nothing lurid in his head,
Though our Shaksperian poet tries to make
His hero with unequalled passion shake;
But as before, when he would make him die
With words upon his lips that reach the sky,

He shows himself a baby at the trade,
In utter helplessness his man to aid;
Here are the dying words of one who drinks
A poison-draught, then lays him down and thinks:
' This is my happy triumph morning; Florence
Is saved; I drink this, and, ere night—die!—strange!'
Indeed, we think he might expect the change.

" Who wishes with precision's eye to see
And know a wit from one that's yet to be,
Let him take *Luria* always in his hand;
With such a manual he will understand
Philosophy of easy play-composing,
Where Love, Despair, and Hope, are ever dozing;
Presumption wide awake, roused by the voice
Of Pride his spouse, whose tongue a scolding choice
Sustains, and tells him, spite of all his show,
He is mean-spirited, afraid to go
And be the haughty general of song,
With SHAKSPERE waiting as his aide-de-camp.

On this Presumption straight leaps out of bed,
Cools in the bath his envy-fevered head,
Forth to his study goes, with all his might
Strives to be foremost in the goose-quill fight.
Alas! when he makes furious advance,
Poising in his right hand the ink-tipped lance,
Dulness' ink-bottle tumbles o'er the page,
Blotting the manuscript, where deadly rage,
With might more fatal than ACHILLES' wrath,
Was to have led him up to glory's path.
In haste Presumption locks his study door,
Lest he should hear of her reproaches more,
Who gives him all the live-long night 'enough of it,'
(To use the BROWNING rhyme; indeed, 'the stuff of it
Is only fit for such a use as this).
But her contemptuous tongue he will not miss;
Presumption at the first may seem most bold,
But Pride his wife, him on her thumb can hold.

'He sighs for fury: 'Ah! for words of flame!'
'Tis true all his are free from arson's blame,

But not if he can help it, for he would
Burn up the earth with language, if he could,
And be with rolling words, like smoke from chimney
    curled,
'The fiery centre of an earthy world.'
But let him go on 'greatening' till he ends,
As he undoubtedly says and intends;
His labours clearly mean to make us see
With evidence of strongest words that he
'The man of men, the spirit of all flesh' is;
Here TENNYSON has had him in his meshes,
Who talks of 'broadening.' Unhappy words!
Ye never sate in good taste's House of Lords;
Your fathers, bred in country villages,
Have never seen the halls of stately bliss,
Where high-born sons spontaneous elegance speak,
And lovely daughters hear with pleasure meek.

    " With what remains we are not better pleased;
'Tis certain his lean reader must have sneezed

O'er BROWNING'S dusty thinking many a time,
For oft his pages seem like clouds of lime,
And as they fall, blown by his wilful breezes,
' He sneezes, twice he sneezes, thrice he sneezes ;'
You will not find this verse, but something like,
Where, eager with fierce emphasis to strike,
' He lies, and twice he lies, and thrice he lies,'
He sings, and sure all truth the third time dies.

" O not a beam of hope shines on our dreary way,
To comfort us with the near break of day ;
Page after page the night succeedeth night,
For Chaos is determined not to take its flight,
Till suddenly we call to mind that we can take the law
At least of BROWNING into our own hands, and draw
Our blinded faculties back to the sun
Of decent order, and with him be done ;
For who with persevering meekness can remain
For any length of time with one from whom comes little
    gain ?

To whom this foolish zeal of soaring speech is given—
'The snail's on the thorn, and God's in His heaven.'
The face of others' thoughts he sucks to skin and bone,
And in this pinched disguise presents it as his own;
And when we meet we say to them, 'You have seen better days
Ere you began to beg for bread on these highways.'

" His *Men and Women* are without a face,
They are all back, there's nothing to embrace;
We travel far to see them, and to learn,
And when from the dull journey we return,
Cry, ' What is a great fight-word?' for, indeed,
We feel pugnacious, ripe a quarrel to breed
With one who leads us through his fens and bogs
Of wordy talk, where we're like hungering dogs,
Whose energies with the vain chase are spent;
Vain chase! what then? he is not worth our scent.

" There's not a penny-a-liner in the land
Who might not easily make a better hand

Of German student life in Göttingen,
Than what he does with his slack-handled pen.
We wander in the wilderness like Jews,
And this lawgiver's counsels justly we refuse;
His wit's unsavoury manna makes us sigh
For Pagans' fleshpots even, with whom to vie
Such Christians shall despair from morn till night;
Their scuttling wings have but the ostrich flight;
Round in word-circles see them wheel and turn,
Their stomachs can stones, wood, and old iron churn
Into a butter for the popular mouth;
But North-bred men laugh at the languid South.

"*Blougram's Apology* is the excuse
Of Bishop BROWNING for his trifling news;
He tries to palliate his being born
Within convenient reach of wine and corn,
And drags in SHAKSPERE to his tavern bar
To help them somewhat in the windpipe war

That BROWNING has with BROWNING o'er his wine;
He hears them talk, who never will combine,
For contradiction is the life of each,
And BROWNING still must unto BROWNING preach.
SHAKSPERE may think, 'Here is a character for me
To play with in the nineteenth century;
Such things could never enter any head
In mine own time, but men have gone to bed
Since then, and this one in some frenzy tries
To find life roaming through his foolscap skies.'

"These books still hold their place 'mong men of sense,
Because they construe in the present tense,
Which for their breakfast is enough, indeed,
As thus, 'I eat;' but past and future need
Construction from a more capacious head
Than his, of whom has been already said
Too much by far; but as he is the type
Of many, 'twould be wrong to spare the stripe,

And he may say again, tied to the mast,
'Surely the bitterness of death is past;'
Then with indignant energy well grogged,
Let our rough quartermaster see him flogged.

"I've oft had pity for the Jewish king
Before whom DAVID sometimes came to sing,
To chase away his melancholy mind,
And give him one of careless pleasure's kind;
But now compassion rises to its height,
When his sad history we see alight
At BROWNING's door, and shelter from him crave,
From Christians' cold neglect its life to save.
When wilful men their minds have rendered dull,
Weary they seek the scolding hours to lull;
To make Time in a seeming stillness lie,
They hasten out into the street and buy
A speaking trumpet at a publisher's,
Through which applause may roar into their ears,
And drown the thundering consciousness of shame,
Which for their parlour thought's the proper name.

To sleekness stroked by ignorant flattery's hand,
They're overjoyed to think that they shall stand
Above their neighbours head and shoulders high;
Soon must they fall on their own swords to die!

"Ten hundred writers should apologise,
That they have been so ignorant and unwise,
With all the wisdom of the past in view,
As not tell BROWNING poems to eschew
As much as JOB shunned evil; they refrain,
For 'tis a wanton thing to speak so plain;
Not one has ventured from his circle out,
For fear and money hold each critic lout;
But most will rage for spite when this they view,
They might have better done, but did not do.

"We counsel him to Nature now to go,
Who will instruct him better thoughts to sow.
Behold him gone; she asks him, 'Who are you?'
'Me, madam? I am one that sips heaven's dew!'

'Not so,' she answers, 'these dry parched lips
Have drunk thought's waters during love's eclipse;
For sound recovery, you must beware
Of living more without my wholesome air:
Leave poetry; some common cabbage prose
Will help you much; beside each house it grows;
It is a dish well suited for the mind;
Sometimes you may its influence windy find,
But never heed the wind, 'twill pass away,
And leave you making stronger every day.
A feeble poet is a pest to me;
I never will encourage such as he;
He talks continually of his great soul,
And all the while it poketh like a mole,
Whose little mounds are useful in their place,
But whom from flower-beds 'tis but wise to chase;
His nostril sensitive and delicate I spurn,
And on his impudence my back I turn."

    Thus far the Muses listened patiently,
Till CUPID, sitting on ERATO's knee,

Grew restless, and desired to go to sleep.
On this they all advised the page to keep
His merry rhymes to serve another day,
When they would farther at this pleasure play.
Low bent the page before the lovely train,
Whose wondrous beauty made his spirit fain;
Then rising, passed into the outer court;
Another page he met, who stopped him short,
Inquiring what commission had been given
That made his face bright with a joy like heaven.
"I have," he said, "in laughing humour uttered
Some words that pleased of a vain man who stuttered
In all his thoughts, yet did not hesitate
To print what's nothing more than idle prate;
A second sermon shall the first succeed,
Mirth following mirth, for of such there is need."
"A sermon should be grave; how then can you
Have hope that Laughter will reveal what's true?"
"O," said the page, "Sermons in stones you'll find,
Why not in pleasantry? 'tis to the mind

A bracing sea-breeze, that restores its spring,
Lost in dark lanes and alleys, where the wing
Of song is soiled by idlers that beguile
Its powers away, and all its grace defile.

> "On Laughter's South-coast line let us to Brighton ride,
> And ocean view once more with a fresh wonder's pride;
> Then turning our regards round quickly to the right,
> With telescope well set, behold the Isle of Wight."

THE LAUGHTER OF THE MUSES.

PART II.

THE LAUGHTER OF THE MUSES.

PART II.—ALFRED TENNYSON.

MORNING in splendour o'er the mansion breaks
Of the fair Nine, and chubby CUPID wakes,
Who all the night upon ERATO's breast
Had lain, enjoying there Love's tranquil rest.
He rubs his eyes, and asks her where's the page
Who yesterday their mirth came to engage.
" He will be here anon," ERATO said,
" Come, smiling PHŒBUS calls thee from thy bed ;
Rise, let us view the morn, sweet Boy of Love,
My sisters walk within the beechen grove,
Let us go too; thy mother comes to-day
From visiting his grave the boar did slay,

Unhappy youth, ADONIS of the chase,
Whose form gave lawless pleasure such a grace,
It made her sigh, and sweat, and wring her hands,
While he, a hunter, rides across the lands.
The boar slew him who slew her chaste desires,
That came too near lust's seven times heated fires.
Now she and you, my sisters and myself
Are under other laws; the ancient delf,
In which young HEBE once the nectar poured,
Is in our mansion's haunted chamber stored.
We take it out at times to satisfy
A curious wish that in the mind will lie;
Its rich designs, its massive workmanship
Can still delight; they make our memories dip
In the clear sparkling streams of past delight,
When love tormented SAPPHO day and night;
When PARIS got a woman for his woe,
And HELEN lost a man to find a foe;
When, cold with love, the sad PENELOPE
Her tempters shunned to sew her tapestry;

When DIDO entertained her pious guest,
And starved herself thereby of nightly rest;
When VESTA was dishonoured by a nun,
And Rome through her, the wondrous Rome, begun;
Like her original, a maid unchaste,
Lavish of favour, who hath long disgraced
The beauty of her holiness. Come, let us hear
Our laughter-loving page; he waits our ear."
ERATO ceased, the youth his verse renewed
Thus in their presence, bashful as he stood:

"O Muses, there is much to tell to-day
Of one who has received the poet's bay,
And by all England has been crowned the king
Of men, and women too, who burn to sing
Till rocks shall dance and trees shall bend around
The magic circle of their little ground.
Applause has danced until she cannot stand,
So now we seek to take her by the hand
And lead her from the close room's heavy air
Into some atmosphere more fresh and fair,

Where she may gather up her powers again,
Profusely wasted among feeble men,
Whose weakness cannot value her rich gifts;
We would construct for her a sieve that sifts
Their 'vacant chaff' of pages, when the wind
Shall blow them back into a place behind,
Where they may lie till padding is required
For other poorhouse poets, who desired
To drink up fame like wine; now, worn and old,
They have not much to shield them from the cold;
They have not where to lay their heads at all,
Though they are still what we must Christians call.
O TENNYSON, and is thy mind the cause
Why thou hast been a gallant to applause?
Thy verses, yield they no more pleasing grace
Than make thee now adorn a needle-case?
Last Saturday I went down Wapping Street,
And passing through the Tunnel, turned my feet
To Cherry Gardens Pier, a steamer took,
The 'Nymph' by name, though sooty was her look.

Upon the starboard paddle-box I read
What made the blood of fancy through my head
More swiftly flow. O surely poets great
Are ever shielded from this puffing fate!
Those magazines that are of world-wide fame,
By dint of blazoning their various name,
Were in this order shown for you to choose—
Lloyd's Weekly, next *Good Words*, last *Sporting News*,
And in the middle *Alfred Tennyson*
In characters of flaming colours shone!
No harm in this. Is there in anything?
No harm in what the Laureate tries to sing;
Yet propped-up poems must soon tumble down,
And on Time's flinty pavement break their crown!

"Grief leads not any up Parnassus' steep;
On hands and knees all crying poets creep;
A joyful note they may catch on the road,
But are they therefore to be called 'the mode'?
If on the whole clouds hide thought's azure sky,
To them the poet's brightness we deny.

His barricades of grief by Joy's strong ram
May be o'erthrown; what's *In Memoriam?*
This image in our mind we've often turned,
A monument of bricks much overburned.
Let's make these pages in their pockets carry
A few to show to youths about to marry
Their thoughts to poetry, how tame the view,
How dull the house of sombre sorrow's hue.

" ' By faith, and faith alone, embrace,' is prose;
' Believing where we cannot prove,' the throes
A poet's mind endures, the verse to end;
' Thine are these orbs'—the writer would unbend
In presence of his Maker, and declare
The wisdom which is spoken everywhere.
The skull is happily placed in HAMLET's hands,
But here 'tis most unpleasing; ifs and ands
Would be more suitable; ' Thou madest Death'
Could only be conceived by one whose breath
Is in his nostrils; to this prelude's end
There's nothing that can make our hopes ascend

Up to the summit of expectant pleasure;
At the hill-foot we may his mind's plot measure.

" ' I held it truth,' just as a mother holds
Her baby; truth must have far wider folds
Than his mind's arms; it is a narrow wit
That cannot start a rhyme with words more fit.

" ' Old Yew!' tell us if his repulsive muse
Would thank thee, or thy grasping rude accuse.
Still on forbidding things he loves to dwell,
Yet nothing says which sextons may not tell;
We seek a poet who will help to hide
Our mortal doom, not one who takes a pride
In skulls and crossbones, holding up to view
The charnel-house in all its ghastly hue;
Though certainly it might be better borne,
Were it not done by language most forlorn.
Not plump and rosy are his words with thought;
From crowded English lanes they have been brought.

"Sorrow has studied for a 'fellowship'
In ALFRED'S college, and no pouting lip
Will ever tempt him from his snug retreat,
But single there he'll warm his icy feet.
What virgin watches in 'the vaults of death'
We cannot tell, for all the poet saith,
But Sorrow she is not, of that we're sure,
For all men think that death of grief's the cure.
'O sweet and bitter in a breath' is gleaned,
And the fourth line of darkness must be cleaned.

"Our generous brother 'gives his powers away
To sleep,' and quite forgets the starving day.
Chaos he makes the master of his will,
And surely he the service doth fulfil.
A young man's death makes rudderless his ship;
How many foundering vessels are let slip
Upon Time's treacherous deep, if this be true!
But we believe he made a helm anew.
'Twas time enough into Song's bay to sail
When he had overblown this whimpering gale.

THE LAUGHTER OF THE MUSES.

" O Poet! thou illusest donkey 'hold;'
For farther service it is now too old.
Do let it go to stretch its legs awhile;
It may perhaps return wearing youth's smile.
O did'st thou never think 'twas a whole sin
'To put in words' thine idle sorrow's din.
Words natural to nature are most like,
But rung by art the soul they never strike;
She sound asleep hears not their feeble knock,
And sleepeth on, door fast with double lock.

" ' One writes' a letter full of common sense,
Which poets hate with a disgust intense;
No common-place can feed their delicate
And sickly stomachs—most unhappy fate!
Alas for them! they must fall to the porridge,
For hunger stirreth up a desperate courage;
And common-place is after all their lot,
For ' vacant chaff well meant for grain' is not
Good prose, but a day-labourer poet's mess,
Or his fond Muse's smothering caress.

"'Dark house by which once more I stand' makes
plain
That grievous things were crowding on his brain
At home and by the way, by night and morn,
In short he was to this same manner born;
And still pursued by the distempered heat,
He paceth up 'the long, unlovely street';
Was't Pompeii? did he not see a man,
That he should place a poet's foolish ban
On all that met his sorrow-jaundiced eyes?
O sir! did not the stones cry out 'Be wise.'
'Tis woman makes a man's heart 'quickly beat;'
His heart is manly when it comes to greet
A brother, or it is diseased and weak;
Love is not wont in such poor terms to speak.

"We do not want to hear in published rhymes
How common lovers are annoyed at times,
As they alight and ring the gateway bell
Where their young charmers with impatience dwell,

THE LAUGHTER OF THE MUSES. 53

When out to them they see the servant come,
Who tells them how the girls are gone from home;
And as a figure, better to rehearse
How one man loves his friend, 'tis worse and worse;
It makes his sorrow very common seem,
Not much illumined by the sacred gleam.

"'Fair ship' from Rome—when Sorrow is Love's
    eye,
'Twill not the most minute details pass by;
His thoughts, like misers, brood upon their gold,
But words, his children, cannot loose his hold
Of the hard coin, that they may now enjoy
In youth the fruits of his whole life's employ.
A beggar's pittance he will only give,
On which they scarcely can afford to live.
But every man is blessed with thinking stuff,
His words, his boys, blab if he has enough
To satisfy his hungering greedy fears,
Which often make him weep despairing tears.

Poet! of silent thought the world's not scant,
But thought in happy speech is what we want.

    "'I hear the noise about thy keel'—all this
Hath never felt imagination's kiss
More than the sailor's merry 'Yo! heave, yo!'
Or carpenter who sings at work below.
The writer writes what anyone could write,
But few would venture forth in such a plight
Without the crutches of applauding friends.
This is but just, for clearly he intends
These rhymes as fanciful, while they are nought
But matter-of-fact inscribed 'for want of thought.'

    "We might expect the 'calm' to change to storm
When it begins to view its rifled form,
And all its stores of sweetness tossed and tumbled,
For him who thought rhymes music when they grumbled.
Calm has a satisfaction in its sound
By itself alone, not when in these thoughts bound.

" No doves spring up to Heaven with tales of woe,
For there all tears for ever cease to flow.
' The wild pulsation' is a wild remark,
For even the dove that flew back to the Ark
Was but excited in a gentle way;
She loitered with an olive leaf to play.
Of ' dolorous messages' she never dreams,
But poets take great licence in their themes.
A crow would yield a too apparent joke,
So to their whirligig a dove they yoke.

" ' Tears of the widower—fall like these '—what's
  here ?
A troubled sea through which Love cannot steer.
He honours widowers: ' O ye wife-bereaved!
Ye grieve like me; after me ye have grieved.'
A husband mourning for a wife deceased
Is not at all in the same manner seized
As when he mourns a friend whom death has taken.
Love will not have her various feelings shaken,

THE LAUGHTER OF THE MUSES.

Her metaphors mixed up in verse laconic,
Prepared like doctor's drugs, for grief a tonic.
Sweet love is thus into vile bitters turned
By one who hath grief's vademecum learned.

"'If one should bring'—when poets fail to sing,
Their prose must be a dry and helpless thing.
They waken up from dreams that grandeur wore,
To hear a servant knocking at the door.
She was the queen that whispered sweetly to them,
But in daylight their visions all eschew them.

"The dropping water hollows out the stone,
And dropping days here make the winds to moan.
The mourner feels the minutes pattering down,
And soiling academic sorrow's gown.
The *Christabel* supplies 'the last red leaf,'
'Rooks blown about' is grain from his thin sheaf,
If our weak ignorance may be so bold
As venture forth from Censure's safe sheepfold.

Praise is a wolf when thought's a wilderness,
Which with the richest flowers and fruits should bless.
Censure's the shepherd driving him away,
Lest on the stupid sheep he seek to prey.

" ' What words are these have fallen from mé?'—
    alas!
If thou know'st not, O poet! we're too crass
To answer thee; hailstones and sleet we shun;
' Sorrow,' ' despair,' ' unrest,'—of them we'll none.

" 'Thou comest much wished for'—no, we do not seek
Dead bodies with desire; this is a freak
Of ill-considered thought, by a design
Begot that reasoned thus: ' Line upon line
Adds to his fame and mine, in chief the last;
Let me with patience have my stanzas cast.'

" ' 'Tis well; 'tis something'—'tis an empty dish
He now serves up—the superficial wish

Of every man to follow to its tomb
The body of a friend; the 'violet's' bloom
Is but a cunning theft of SHAKSPERE'S 'bung,'
Who so of mighty CÆSAR'S carcase sung.
The borrower's flushing cheek denies the charge,
But spite of that we wait not to enlarge.

"We must more quickly turn these pages o'er;
Already CUPID hath begun to snore.
Too much of the same thing your ears will tire,
And for the rest leave only spent desire.
Then through the blubbering verses let us hurry,
That we may other songs in frolic worry.
To your glad wisdom 'tis superfluous
For me to plod through every section thus.
If you receive what I've said hitherto,
And give assent to humour's first review,
We need not follow orderly the course;
Let's give the reins to our gay prancing horse,
That he may range through all the poet's plains,
Sniffing the breeze, and hunting what remains.

THE LAUGHTER OF THE MUSES.

And should we 'vex the poet's mind' at all,
He has the right this 'shallow wit' to call;
If weak, 'twill vex him in a pleasant way;
If strong, 'twill please him though his foe says nay;
Therefore we say to all who read these lines,
When they would sing beneath their peaceful vines:
'Pull not down the window blinds where a poet sits,
For there the sunshine comes and finds him " warming
    his five wits." '

"'When in the down'—the rhymer's downy grief
Supports him far beyond his own belief.
Such vivid picture we have never read
Of pillows comforting a poet's head.
But Sleep,* good sir, was born in Paradise,
And after that Death dropped from blacker skies.
He pilfers madly out of mad *Queen Mab*,
And in the dark makes but a random stab

---

* Tennyson twice in this stanza calls Sleep the twin-brother of Death.

At ghostly figures rising in his sleep,
While they afraid a cautious distance keep.
When one makes it a hard task to conceive,
To him it is not easy; he should leave
The work alone, for it succeeds much better
When freed from pride's close cell and clanking fetter.

" ' I hold it true' begins a verse whose sense
Is in its sound; with agony immense
He cries, ' 'tis better to have loved and lost
Than never to have loved at all'—poor boast
That has no meaning; love is ever found,
And never lost upon a poet's ground.
Was he from trammels loosed of time and place,
When this thin-visaged fancy showed its face?
It is not truth, and therefore 'tis not song;
To every day such common things belong.
'Tis but self-flattery, which hath no aim
Save only double righteousness to claim.
Are 'loved' and 'lost' foes here of the same stature?
Then hath the author all mistook their nature.

THE LAUGHTER OF THE MUSES.

If thou hast loved and lost, O TENNYSON,
There's not a poorer man the earth upon.
But without thought thou writest, we believe,
And wip'st thy quill upon thine own coat-sleeve,
Which is a proof of carelessness and haste,
And these have often lovely minds defaced.
They should be driven out of Love's domains,
Where Summer over fertile valleys reigns.

" What is the *Princess* we need not inquire,
For she is called a '*Medley*' by her sire,
And 'twould be vain and foolish to gainsay
What he has said so fitly of his lay.
The words 'weird seizure' he at intervals
Brings to his aid when recollection calls,
But the design is plain, to lift the mind
From heaps of prosy blank, by the trade-wind
Of an imagination that we're sure
Will never take us far from our own door.
There is a story of a bandit chief,
Who for concealment, lest the doom of thief

Should fall on him, pretended to be lame,
When he would go where his housebreaking fame
For him was dangerously remembered still,
Where men would seize him with a hearty will.
One day he entered Paris, and awhile
Went through the streets unmindful of his guile,
When suddenly remembering he should limp,
He of deception made himself the pimp,
And halted all at once upon the street;
A gendarme hastened up the man to greet,
And make of him a sharp and stern inquiry
What pain had caught his limb but late so wiry.
So our policeman is not slow to see
That 'weird' and TENNYSON don't well agree.

"His words are pocket-knives worn to the handles,
Or like to in the desert used up sandals
Strapped to the feet of his weary pilgrim mind,
That strives in distant Islam realms to find
What may be found at home with love's light trouble;
To search for beauty is to find a bubble.

THE LAUGHTER OF THE MUSES.

Fulness of thought has never cause to seek,
And only for delight will care to speak.
His 'golden,' 'glimmering,' 'silver,' 'flower,' 'eclipse,'
Have worn all beauty from his thinking lips;
They're like to Gibeonites, with garments torn and glazed,
At which all the king's daughters are amazed;
They ask him where's his glorious apparel,
And why he comes such an impoverished carle.

"The owl songs can be sung but by an owl,
And after COLERIDGE only make us howl;
'Divinest'* memory is from the same received,
And of his rights he must not be bereaved.
'With golden stars above' is very poor,
Nor can the common sense of song endure
Such flights as 'hate of hate' and 'scorn of scorn,'
And 'love of love,' which beggars wait forlorn

---

* Coleridge sings "Divinest Liberty" in his youthful ode on France.

Before the wealthy mansions of the Muses,
Whose love to them all charity refuses.
The poet cannot see through 'good and ill,'
Nor does he know 'the everlasting will.'

" What melancholy must have vexed his soul
In thinking on his broken golden bowl,
How men will come and hold their orgies round
His tomb, unhallowing the sacred ground.
O Poet! and art thou so much afraid
Of scandalous cries, when in the earth thou'rt laid ?
Be not offended, for thou wilt not hear
What shakes thee with such sentimental fear;
To publish such vain drivelling as this
Deserveth not our laughter's frown to miss.
That men he thinks want music in their ears
Will delve about his grave and shed no tears;
But, tearing off his papier-maché shroud,
Hold up his heart in scorn before the crowd.
His 'sounder leaf' will not enbalm his fame;
Of fitting speech such poverty's a shame.

He claimeth SHAKSPERE by the poorest lines
And doubtfullest that may be gathered from his mines;
Heaven grant that this may lead to nothing worse
Than to be under such a powerless curse.
And with the Irishman cursed by his priest
We would exclaim, ere from this song we've ceased:
' Well, well, I fear not, for I've come to know
How far your cursing 'gainst my soul can go.'

"' Break, break,' might answer once upon a day,
But SHAKSPERE'S ' Blow, blow,' blows it quite away.
It lies within thought's most restricted power
To make such simple copies once an hour:
Jump, jump, O Hapless girl, from London Bridge,
Thy spirit's mountain is vexed by a midge;
Clean, clean, O Shoeblack, all the boots you can,
For you are happier than a richer man;
Drive, drive thy 'bus, O Coachman, to the Bank,
The jolly man is not above thy rank.
When sorrow is too garrulous, we wish
That it would leap away and be a fish,

Leave its dull crags, and mingle with the sea,
For grief that talks so much must silly be;
And after we have been well crammed with woes,
We find in laughing at them a repose.

"*The Miller's Daughter* hath a foolish song,
That never should to manhood true belong:
What love-sick youth could ever wish t' appear
A jewel hanging at a lady's ear?
Would she have him as girdle to her waist,
Or necklace lying on her bosom chaste?
Yet this is the whole song—a song indeed
Tuned to the rules of an effeminate creed.
The other, 'Love that hath us in the net,'
We quickly hear, and quickly we forget;
The rhyme might answer for a playground wall,
At which we throw each line like tennis-ball.

"*Maud* is a battered, bruised, and flattened tale,
Composed when mad thought's equinoctial gale

Raged with a turbid vehemence in his breast,
And kept him from his six hours' needful rest.
'Twas written in a frenzy, not, take heed,
Of finest quality ; resolved to bleed
Imagination well, at every pore
He held his basin, losing not a drop
Of precious life, till weakness made him stop.
It is a harvest where good grain is scant,
For he would reap where he forgot to plant;
An uncleansed mixture, weedy through and through,
Each section is held prominent to view ;
But all the pauses might be blotted out,
And not affect what he's so wild about.
O Muses, there is nothing here to stop our mirth;
We shall be grave when he sings something worth.
There is no time to spend on *Maud's* mad lay ;
With this one word we pass from her away:
'For he had many,[*] poor worm' is so common,
That it might readily have struck a woman.

---

[*] Alluding to the numerous rings his rival wore.

"To his satirical attempt we turn:
We know not if he has resolved to burn—
'No coarser frog e'er croaked in Helicon,' *
Which shows the muse of ALFRED TENNYSON
Doth bathe in stagnant water, lazy maid,
To be content in such green ponds to wade,
And not ascend the hill to purer springs!
If to this standing wit the poet clings
No longer, but regretfully withdraws
Its leg, to him who quotes it 'mongst his laws,
We still may speak, the critic MATTHEW named,
Whose 'Culture' must by 'Anarchy' be claimed.

"And what are *Lilian, Isabel, Madeline?*
They have no elegance, nor do they shine
In love's bright morning rays, and freedom's grace,
The life of world-wide song, we fail to trace.

---

* Compare Burns:
    "O were I on Parnassus' hill,
    And drank of Helicon my fill."

Troops of strained epithets, that come pell-mell
After each other, with great labour tell
The truth concerning girls; believe it, none
Can be convinced to love of any one
More strongly than before by these hard names,
Which are not flattering to graceful dames.
Who doubts if woman's nature shows a field
That can with ease far richer beauties yield,
By the first comer to be gathered first,
But not by one whose mind is parched by thirst
Instinctive self-love ever must produce,
Which love can only hold a few years' truce
With love's grand sentiment, that overlooks
The mind's great deep, where poets' little brooks,
That sometimes think their stream's enough to fill
And water all earth's ridges, empty will
Themselves and there be lost for ever.
An ocean cannot dwindle to a river;
A poet should not sink into a lover,
Or magnify a woman; let him hover

Around, above her beauty, that his lyre
May yield in songs harmonious his desire.
'Black-beaded' we have seen in pictures praised;
A maiden's eyes by this are not much raised;
A faulty figure angry makes our minds,
And with its presence better fancies blinds.
To make their eyes like beads makes women dolls;
Such meagre praise no dark-eyed girl cajoles.
The metre of the song is wholly spoiled
By *Lili-an,* which looks as if he puffed and toiled
To drag it up to melody's hill top,
But half-way down he had to let it drop.

" He sends to one a sort of allegory,
Which is a feeble, strangely worded story.
He calls a wicked man a 'glorious devil;'
If to a man he is so wondrous civil,
What shall he say of SATAN? 'power of brain,'
That feeds upon itself becomes inane.
When words are pampered by uxorious love,
In tyrant fretfulness they sit above

The thoughtless wooer, who can never please,
Though he has worshipped them upon his knees.
Description in his hands is torn to shreds;
He gathers docks from amaranthine beds;
' Sheeny ' and all the rest are schoolboy's plums
He eats when to his sixteenth year he comes.

" I heard a Scottish clergyman repeat
What he appeared to think with truth was sweet:
' Peace like a universal shaft of light
Across the land,' which fails in meaning quite,
For ' shafts of light ' are local; I opine,
He'd squeeze the universe into a line
With his tremendous figures, but too much
His greed's imagination tries to clutch.
' The circle of the golden year ' must fail
O'er ' golden age,' its parent, to prevail.

" The *Idylls* cannot yield so much to please
As fiddles strung and tuned by one at ease

With his own mind and all the world beside.
Thoughts well expressed here stand asunder wide,
And these but repetitions of the past,
True fancy seemeth wholly overcast,
Imagination seldom works at all;
It must have had a long and serious brawl
With former poets, and come off defeated;
'Tis a pet lamb that never leaped and bleated
Among the mountains, but nursed by the fire
Of jog-trot thought, looks singed and confident.

" Now think we it is time away we went
From verses blank, and finish up our story,
Leaving the *Brook* to publish forth his glory,
Which has in truth a prettiness of rhyme,
Yet only can with shallow fancies chime,
That chatter, chatter, as they flow to join life's **brimming river**;
For brooks may come and brooks may go, but men go on for ever.

"'Tis his misfortune to be counted great;
No wonder he to keep up noble state
Finds it a difficult and weary matter,
And sighs, 'Would Fame, like CASSIUS, were fatter!'
Envy barks round him with its wretched noise,
And all his powers to ward it off employs,
When if he would be dumb 'twould be much better
Than give to *Once-a-Week* 'a spiteful letter,'
Where he, some say, takes his assailant's part,
And tells him of his rhododendron heart.

"When helplessness of speech is placed in front,
It must of cuts and slashes bear the brunt;
All those behind learn to be helpless too,
For idle work's an easy think to do,
And daily seems more easy; so they lie,
Nor will they make an effort thought to try.
Thus day by day their spirits thinner grow,
Till authors past can scarce the present know.
The former still are strong and rich with youth;
Though ghosts, they are the happy ghosts of truth;

The latter, though alive, are weak and old,
And shiver at the thought of future cold,
When they shall pass away from mortal strife
For love, gold, fame, to the all-glorious life.

" Upon the stepping stones that we have made
Of TENNYSON and BROWNING, for whose aid
We are most grateful, let us try to gain
An eminence commanding England's plain,
Where myriad hearts are glad with silent love
They feel is theirs, and need not words to prove.

" Now look around and view the degradation
Of heavenly speech throughout this Christian nation;
See heaps of monstrous and deluding tales,
As plentifully made as cotton bales;
No scruples felt by publishers or hacks,
While critics advertise the stuff like quacks.
Sensation's made a prostitute for gold,
Tricked out in flaunting phrases to be sold;

THE LAUGHTER OF THE MUSES.

She walks about among the high and low,
And to salute her boldness few are slow;
The paper lords that have the public ear
Familiar chuck her on the chin, and leer
With winks of knowledge; all her joys they've shared
In secret, now they see with bosom bared
The wanton driven forth into the street,
To make up with the first youth she may meet.
They never had a true affection for her,
So all the joy she gave is turned to horror.

"Since feeble-minded authors took their seats
High in Fame's halls, where their false genius cheats;
Since an outlandish man in hob-nailed shoes
Came stumping to the South to tell his news;
Since poetry fell down into the mud;
Since Protestants began to chew the cud
Of Popery, when they in empty stalls
Were standing, to an outhouse genius thralls,
This land of freedom hath become enslaved,
And she must change before she can be saved;

For liberty is for the child of might,
That is the only true eternal right.
These roaring writers think their minds are strong;
The world awakes to tell them they are wrong!
Might is man's right, but where, oh where, is might?
Not in what such originals can write.
Many write nobly, but in terror's chains;
To banish ranting fools they take no pains.
Men pusillanimous stand in life's breach,
But they are frightened by a night-owl's screech;
They turn and cry, 'Work, work,' which means 'Fly,
    fly!'
'Come not up here, or ye shall surely die!'
Joy's citadel is not for men so scurvy,
Who with their fears would turn earth topsy-turvy.

"Men women these have made, and women men;
One felt herself so little of a hen,
That she, a would-be chanticleer of truth,
Was not content with Mary, Jane, or Ruth,

But took, 'tis said, a man's own proper name,
And there was not a voice to chide the same.
To throw away a woman's wondrous grace,
Is to make Nature's beauty hide its face.

" O Mansion of the tenderest thoughts of earth!
Still let thy halls resound with gentle mirth;
Still let desire sing her sweet melodies,
Who, waked by love, her pleasure cannot miss,
For love is life's most ravishing content,
And woman's heart love's sweetest instrument
That can be heard throughout these earthly seats
Where Nature's beauty powerfully entreats
Our sense, but lovely woman charms the soul,
Whose pining love by her is oft made whole,
While time afflicts with heaviness of mind,
Striving to reach thoughts not of earthly kind.
Still, Woman, let thy fancies make thee fair,
Thine eyes refuse man's glances bold to wear,
For he best learneth modesty from thee,
And if not thou, who shall his tutor be?

Much needed now, since he is left alone,
And snarling stoops to pick Disdain's bare bone.
Wisdom and you he leaveth to survey
With blinking eyes the traces of his clay,
That may beneath the delved earth be found,
As if his foresight sought a spot of ground
Where he through all eternity may hide.
But his forefathers did not so divide
Their greater time; they in the morning rose,
When Sunrise with a virgin's brightness glows,
And catching from its beams a lively joy,
They shone, nor could earth's shadows them annoy.

"Now some would dress themselves in heathen rags,
Make life a cauldron, stirring there like hags
Care's hellbroth mixed by hurtful pleasure's hand,
Offering 't to youths too strong to understand.
Now some are plastered o'er with whitening light;
A gairish wisdom makes their faces bright.

Now women make a wisdom of their own,
By which they hope to gain dominion's throne;
False teachers flatter them in all their ways,
Until they are to ordinary praise
At home insensible: they too must write,
And leave the nursery and needle quite.
For they have found that men are feminine,
Whose minds on grief's hodge-podge of language dine;
Weak they must ever stoop to sorrow's trifles,
And joy's vast wealth its sobbing never stifles.
They whine so wofully, the world turns round,
And wonders much at the impertinent sound.

"What wants the world with their bedchamber
    groans,
Coaxing their misery, like lazy drones,
To speak for them, and beg all passers by
That they come in and see them where they lie.
What do they see? Nought which affection moves,
But men whom every working man reproves.

Women will spurn their cowardice, we hope,
Though now led by its lies, they pine and mope,
Impatient with themselves, their idle lords,
Who dangle in the drawing-room their swords,
And simper forth with soft affected drawl
Their empty songs; ladies, a Cashmere shawl
Is better far than all that they can teach;
Let us admire you in't, and let them preach.
They never understood your loveliness,
Hence all they say you find to be a mess
Of pride and ignorance mixed; they cannot love you,
So vainly shall they try to sit above you.
They sometimes try contempt, which is a poor
And stupid way of finding your heart's door,
Like a policeman mean enough to stoop
And cuff a happy boy trundling his hoop,
Not like a chevalier, exulting wise
To praise the splendour beaming from your eyes;
For, sunk themselves, they would degrade you too,
But this, thank Love, they lack the power to do.

THE LAUGHTER OF THE MUSES.

"Women depend on men who love them most,
Deserting those who make their love mere boast,
Who show no independence save a pride
True love and woman ever make us hide.
Now the dependent, free from Love's control,
Leave men alone and act like natures whole;
Placed on a level with their natural kings,
They think and judge even as their fancy sings.
They now arrange their beauties as they please
Whose aim is how unwary youth to seize.

"Why is it crowds to theatres resort?
Not with a genuine playful wit to sport,
Not with the wish to elevate their thought
By cheerful mirth in vain they've elsewhere sought.
What see they on the stage but dramas wan,
So weak, 'tis wonderful they lure a man.
Nor do they, but from Fashion's seats men drink
Draughts with their eyes; mothers have come to think
Low-trimmed attire on lovely girls of twenty
Makes them like overflowing horns of plenty;

But more display more poverty discovers,
Which drives into disgust awakened lovers.
Let them shut to the silken doors again,
If they the faith of men would still retain.

" Is it because the ruling thinkers spoil
True grace, pouring in vain on passion's blazing oil
Rhyme's water, that ye turn away in scorn,
Refusing to submit to minds so worn?
Is it because their verses yield no food
To strengthen your desires to follow good?

" These cooks in genius' palaces prepare
Poetic dinners, while their masters are
Departed to the vast eternal shore,
From whose dread calm they shall return no more
Into the human city's echoing streets;
Their servants left run riot 'mong the meats
Their lords found insufficient to remove
The sickness caused by poverty of love.

They try so hard to occupy the seats
Of COLERIDGE, WORDSWORTH, BYRON, SHELLEY, KEATS,
Filling their bellies, not their minds, with song,
Their revels into midnight they prolong,
Till, drunken, their identity they lose,
And utter nonsense that can scarce amuse.
Their vain ignoble faces soon betray
They only mimic each his master's way.
They shall not find the wisdom of the wise
In all these various climbers to the skies;
Those only find it who have learned to guage
By highest wisdom thoughts of every age,
Who have been taught all things to see as good,
And know how to convert all into food.
Against the truth there's nothing can be done,
And from deceiving words truth may be won;
But fools will praise the folly of the fool,
And take it up their foolish life to rule.

"As men of wealth are all alike to knaves;
As of gay dress a thoughtless woman raves;

As women are alike to hypocrites;
And sermons to the intellect of wits.;
Philosophers to Gospel Pharisees;
And publicans to those who pray with ease,
So poets are all one to humdrum folks,
Whose daily meditations tick like clocks,
Who look at them as they at proverbs look—
Good sayings curiously bound in a book.

"But the humdrum from poets need not shrink,
For what are poets? men who eat and drink.
Why should they not like other people be,
When they have reason none, that we can see,
To be unlike; their hands have fingers five,
They walk at large, and often learn to thrive;
They value gold as much as other men,
And a good bargain's not beneath their ken.

"Then, ye proud sons of rhyme, your poet's nose
Need not be upturned when a child of prose,

A plain religious man, makes up to you,
And by your side takes a contented view
Of women, men, and things in general,
Which nearly yours resembles, after all.
And ye who prose prefer, turn not away,
When some poor lovers try to make you gay
By setting down in order human words,
Whose grace, it has been proved, great joy affords.

" But let them not be petty 'imps of fame,'
Who would with discontentment's greed lay claim
To the wide universe of thought and speech,
Whose tongues aye rage like the bloodthirsty leech,
And never say, ' It is enough for us
That we may speak, unlike the martyred HUSS,
Dowered with a freedom to repeat the truth
That comes to us in everlasting youth;
More have we than we need to occupy
The threescore years and ten before we die.'

"Within the Courts of Song there is a rabble,
Who of the great, SHAKSPERE and MILTON, gabble;
They praise the force of their aspiring powers,
But their own wisdom 'bove these poets towers,
Who never were ashamed their faith to own,
While modern Shaksperes let all faiths alone.
Their praise of genius is a razor keen
That cuts their throats; such suicide is mean.
Some gather skulls as children gather shells,
But where's the soul that in these temples dwells
They never ask, for it unseen remains,
And by the visible they're held in chains."

The Page here ended with a willing mind,
And went away with face to earth declined.
The Muses and their guests, the Queen of Love,
And CUPID, rising left the shady grove,
Over whose roof Night's gathering shadows hung,
While from her unseen hand sweet dews were flung.
They, passing through the porch, into the hall
Entered to sup: nine pages wait their call.

THE LAUGHTER OF THE MUSES.

CUPID that night the chief seat occupied.
On him the Virgin Sisters looked with pride
As their adopted heir, whose youthful smile
And joy untiring every day beguile.
Soon rose they all, and sought with glad desire
Their several chambers, where Sleep's lulling choir
Soothes them into a blessed tranquillity,
That comes to love each evening constantly.

Upon his couch the Page, too, lay and dreamed:
A company of travellers round him seemed
To circle, who would have him, right or wrong,
Repeat from first to last his hasty song.
He had no power their wishes to refuse,
And sang to them as to his sovereign Muse.

The Page awoke; the travellers were gone;
He, lying, his glad thoughts resumed alone,
And spake aloud straight as the fancies came,
For thoughts and words to him were much the same:

"I see one man with peevish anger frowning,
Because I've tried to speak the truth of BROWNING;
I hear another cry, 'It is ill done
To laugh so loud at laurelled TENNYSON.'
One threw his flattering quill into the fire;
Another tore his proof-sheets in his ire,
Sheets filled with 'studies' of the popular man;
One gentle soul approved the satire's plan,
But not a word said in its praise at all,
For on his time he had a stronger call.
He had arisen from rhyme's alluring charms
Foolish, like SAMSON from DELILAH'S arms,
And wandered forth into the open air
To shake himself, and feel his growing hair
Bring back his wonted strength, which he would use
In overthrowing Dagons and their crews."

"Seek not for love among the Philistines,"
He cries, "deep ditches are they, treacherous mines;
Gath is their faith and Askelon their pride;
Their poem-idols have the truth defied;

Their words are but uncharitable libel,
To find the truth turn to the Holy Bible.
They sent the Ark of GOD back to its place,
But they must thither come to plead their case,
For unto them it shall no more return
Who sought to make it of pure creeds the urn.
And trust not the backsliding Israelites,
Who hanker after Hinnom's bloody rites,
Philosophy's high places, Science' hill,
And under green trees sit of human skill.
Trust no one, nor salute him as a prince
Whose conscience day by day doth make him wince;
Trust all, and greet them as a race of kings
And queens, whom love to earth each moment brings."

FINIS.

Titles in this Series

Criticism: General, Poetic, and Dramatic

1. Alfred Austin. THE POETRY OF THE PERIOD. 1870

2. Robert Buchanan. A LOOK ROUND LITERATURE. 1887

3. John William Cole. THE LIFE AND THEATRICAL TIMES OF CHARLES KEAN, F.S.A. 1859.
   (In two volumes)

4. E. S. Dallas. POETICS: AN ESSAY ON POETRY. 1852

5. E. S. Dallas. THE GAY SCIENCE. 1866

6. H. Buxton Forman. OUR LIVING POETS: AN ESSAY IN CRITICISM. 1871

7. Walter Hamilton. THE AESTHETIC MOVEMENT IN ENGLAND, third edition, 1882

8. R. H. Horne, editor. A NEW SPIRIT OF THE AGE, second edition. 1844. (In two volumes)

9. Madge Kendall. THE DRAMA. 1884. with DRAMATIC OPINIONS. 1890

10. Joseph A. Knight. A HISTORY OF THE STAGE DURING THE VICTORIAN ERA. 1901

11. Lord William Pitt Lennox. PLAYS, PLAYERS, AND PLAYHOUSES AT HOME AND ABROAD. 1881.
    (In two volumes)

12. Robert James Mann. TENNYSON'S "MAUD" VINDICATED: AN EXPLANATORY ESSAY. 1856

13. Mowbray Morris. ESSAYS IN THEATRICAL CRITICISM. 1882

14. Henry Neville. THE STAGE: ITS PAST AND PRESENT IN RELATION TO FINE ART. 1875

15. "Q" [Thomas Purnell]. DRAMATISTS OF THE PRESENT DAY. 1871

16. Walter Raleigh. STYLE. 1897

17. William Caldwell Roscoe. POEMS AND ESSAYS (volume two, ESSAYS, only). 1860

18. Clement Scott. THE DRAMA OF YESTERDAY & TODAY. 1899. (In two volumes)

19. James Field Stanfield. AN ESSAY ON THE STUDY AND COMPOSITION OF BIOGRAPHY. 1813

Parody, Satire, Literary Controversy, and Curiosa

20. Edward Bulwer-Lytton. THE NEW TIMON. 1846. with Algernon Charles Swinburne. SPECIMENS OF MODERN POETS. THE HEPTALOGIA, OR THE SEVEN AGAINST SENSE. 1880. with Algernon Charles Swinburne. "DISGUST: A DRAMATIC MONOLOGUE." 1898

21. [William E. Aytoun and Theodore Martin.] THE BOOK OF BALLADS: EDITED BY BON GAULTIER. 1845. with [William E. Aytoun.] FERMILIAN: OR THE STUDENT OF BADAJOZ: A SPASMODIC TRAGEDY BY T. PERCY JONES. 1854

22. James Carnegie. JONAS FISHER: A POEM IN BROWN AND WHITE. 1875. with [A. C. Swinburne.] THE DEVIL'S DUE: A LETTER TO THE EDITOR OF "THE EXAMINER." BY THOMAS MAITLAND. 1875

23. Philip James Bailey. THE AGE; A COLLOQUIAL SATIRE. 1858

24. [W. C. Bennett.] ANTI-MAUD. 1865. with [Eustace Clare Grenville Murray.] THE COMING K———. 1873. with [W. H. Mallock.] EVERY MAN HIS OWN POET. 1877

25. [John Burley Waring.] POEMS INSPIRED BY CERTAIN PICTURES AT THE ART TREASURES EXHIBITION, MANCHESTER. 1857. with [Anon.] THE LAUGHTER OF THE MUSES. 1869

26. Robert Buchanan. THE FLESHLY SCHOOL OF POETRY AND OTHER PHENOMENA OF THE DAY. 1872. with Algernon Charles Swinburne. UNDER THE MICROSCOPE. 1872

27. J. Rutter. THE NINETEENTH CENTURY, A POEM, IN TWENTY-NINE CANTOS. 1900

Collections of Critical Essays

28. William E. Fredeman, editor. VICTORIAN PREFACES AND INTRODUCTIONS: A FACSIMILE COLLECTION. 1986

29. Ira Bruce Nadel, editor. VICTORIAN FICTION: A COLLECTION OF ESSAYS FROM THE PERIOD. 1986

30. Ira Bruce Nadel, editor. VICTORIAN BIOGRAPHY: A COLLECTION OF ESSAYS FROM THE PERIOD. 1986

31. John F. Stasny, editor. VICTORIAN POETRY: A COLLECTION OF ESSAYS FROM THE PERIOD. 1986

32. William E. Fredeman, editor. THE VICTORIAN POETS: AN ALPHABETICAL COMPILATION OF THE BIO-CRITICAL INTRODUCTIONS TO THE VICTORIAN POETS FROM A. H. MILES'S "THE POETS AND POETRY OF THE NINETEENTH CENTURY." 1986

LIBRARY OF DAVIDSON COLLEGE

Books on regular loan may be checked out for **two weeks**. Books must be presented at the Circulation Desk in order to be renewed.

A fine is charged after date due.

Special books are subject to special regulations at the discretion of the library staff.